This book is printed in the United States of America and distributed worldwide.

First Edition: 2023

For information, please contact the author through the publisher.

Amazon Kindle Direct Publishing
Seattle, WA
www.amazon.com/kdp

A portion of all sales from this work will go to numerous charities

"The Greatest Endeavors: Records that Test the Limits of Human Resilience" invites you on an incredible journey of discovery, where human resilience knows no bounds. Uncover six riveting true stories, each serving as a testament to the indomitable human spirit. 'The Greatest Endeavors' is not just a book; it is an inspiring expedition that will set alight your resolve, stoke your motivation, and challenge your understanding of your own boundaries."

The Greatest Endeavors
By George E. Henry
First Edition

"Frozen Triumph - Sir Ernest Shackleton and His Crew - 1914"

In 1914, under the frosty sky of the Antarctic and amid a biting wind that could freeze the marrow in your bones, Sir Ernest Shackleton and his crew of twenty-seven men set forth on an audacious quest. Their mission was no less than to cross the vast, ice-clad expanse of Antarctica, aiming to tread where no man had ever set foot. The ship aptly named the Endurance was their fortress, their home, and their lifeline in this desolate landscape.

In January 1915, the Endurance found herself ensnared in the iron-like grip of floating ice in the Weddell Sea. They were like mice in the jaws of an icy cat, powerless against the freezing tendrils reaching for them. As winter settled in, the ice tightened its clench, embedding the ship deep in its frozen heart. Despite the dire situation, Shackleton's spirit was indomitable. He orchestrated a rigorous routine of games, dog sledding, and hunting to maintain morale. Every day, his eyes met the horizon with a gleam of quiet defiance.

The icy stranglehold lasted ten months before the inevitable happened. In November 1915, the ruthless Antarctic ice, indifferent to their human struggle, finally crushed the Endurance. It was a slow death; an agonizing display of the ship's timbers splintering, creaking, and finally giving in to the merciless ice.

Stranded on the ice with meager provisions and three lifeboats, the men had a battle of survival ahead. Shackleton, standing tall against the immense white backdrop, made a simple but powerful declaration, "Ship and stores have gone – so now we'll go home." Their mission had evolved from an expedition to a battle for survival.

As the ice floe they camped on began to disintegrate, Shackleton ordered a daring escape in the lifeboats to the uninhabited

Elephant Island. The men, weary and frostbitten, cheered weakly as they finally stepped on solid ground after 497 days.

But they were still over 800 miles away from civilization, isolated from the rest of the world. Shackleton, gaunt but unbroken, decided to embark on a rescue mission. With five volunteers, he launched a 22-foot lifeboat, the James Caird, on a desperate voyage across one of the world's most treacherous stretches of water, to South Georgia.

In the face of towering waves and gales that could toss their small boat like a toy, they navigated by the stars. Shackleton's unyielding will was their compass. After seventeen days of being battered by the elements, their salt-crusted eyes spotted the jagged peaks of South Georgia.

However, joy gave way to a grim realization. They had landed on the uninhabited side of the island. Unfazed, Shackleton, along with two others, decided to cross the glacier-ridden landscape on foot to reach the whaling station on the other side. The odds were stacked against them, yet they fought through crevasses, frostbite, and fatigue.

Thirty-six hours later, their frostbitten faces appeared at the Stromness whaling station. The station master stared at these apparitions in disbelief before offering them warm hospitality. The first leg of their rescue mission was a success.

Shackleton wasted no time and coordinated a rescue operation to save his crew stranded on Elephant Island. After four attempts and over three months, Shackleton aboard the Chilean ship Yelcho finally reached the beleaguered men. He found them all alive, their spirit unbroken.

Through the bold leadership of Shackleton, the Endurance crew survived nearly two years in the inhospitable landscape of the Antarctic. As they boarded the Yelcho, their hearts echoed with an unspoken sense of triumph. Shackleton stood among his men, his eyes welling up with pride and relief, his mission finally complete.

As they sailed away from the icy shores of Antarctica, the men took one last look at the desolate wilderness that had been their home for so long. Behind them lay a tale of human endurance and resilience that would be etched in history forever.

Every obstacle they faced was met with an iron will that refused to yield, every peril defied with unwavering resolve, and every hopeless dawn met with a renewed spirit. They hadn't just survived the Antarctic, they had challenged it, bested it, and had come out the other side stronger than they had ever been.

Shackleton's Endurance expedition didn't achieve its initial objective of crossing Antarctica. Yet, it achieved something far more profound. It became an incredible testament to human resilience, leadership, and the indomitable spirit of man in the face of overwhelming adversity.

In the heart of the Antarctic, the crew of the Endurance found something that transcended geographical discovery: they discovered their invincible spirit. They discovered that within each one of them was an unyielding force of endurance that could conquer even the harshest trials that life had to offer.

And so, Shackleton's expedition became a beacon of hope and resilience, a symbol of unwavering courage in the face of despair. Today, it serves as a timeless reminder of the boundless potential that lives within every human spirit. We all have an Antarctic to conquer, an Endurance expedition to embark upon, and within us all, the strength to overcome.

The legacy of Sir Ernest Shackleton and his crew's incredible survival story continues to inspire us to face our challenges head-on, encouraging us to dig deeper, to not just endure our personal trials, but to emerge victorious. For in the end, it's not the adversity but how we face it that truly defines us.

"The Boulder's Grip - Aron Ralston - 2003"

The sun was high in the Utah sky on April 26, 2003, when Aron Ralston, an experienced outdoorsman and a passionate adventurer, began his solitary expedition into the remote Blue John Canyon. Armed with his sturdy climbing gear and a love for the outdoors that had been his lifelong companion, Ralston was drawn to the uncharted territories, the solitude, and the untamed wild that Mother Nature had to offer. However, on this particular journey, nature had a harsh lesson in store for him, one that would test the limits of his courage, endurance, and will to survive.

Ralston began his day by skimming through the narrow, winding paths, the unique contours of the desert's sandstone landscape guiding his journey. His heart was light, his spirits high; he reveled in the fierce freedom that only such vast and untamed surroundings could offer. But as he navigated deeper into the rugged terrains of the canyon, an unforeseen danger lurked around the corner.

While descending into one of the narrow slots of the canyon, a

dislodged boulder crashed onto his right arm, pinning it against the

unyielding canyon wall. His initial shock quickly turned into a surge

of adrenaline as he attempted to free his arm, his cries of

frustration and alarm echoing eerily against the desolate canyon

walls.

However, his efforts bore no fruit; the formidable boulder refused

to budge, and his arm remained trapped. As the harsh reality of his

situation set in, Ralston was faced with a daunting task - a test of

survival in an unforgiving wilderness. With only a small amount of

water and two burritos for sustenance, he prepared himself for the

ordeal that lay ahead.

Days turned into nights, and nights into days. The once beautiful

sunlit canyon that Ralston admired was now a freezing trap, a

relentless reminder of his plight. He was surrounded by the vast,

majestic beauty of nature, but the once liberating solitude of the

desert now taunted his dire predicament. With each passing day, his hopes of rescue dwindled as he came to grips with a terrifying possibility: he might not get out alive.

Ralston documented his harrowing experience through a video diary on his camera, leaving poignant messages for his family. His physical condition deteriorated as dehydration and starvation took hold, but his determination remained unscathed. In his darkest moments, he chipped away at the boulder, rigged pulleys, and even attempted to amputate his arm with a dull knife from his multi-tool.

On the fifth day, with no water left and a grim acceptance of his looming death, Ralston's desperation fueled a moment of sheer grit and resolve. He saw a vision of a little boy, his future son, spurring him into a renewed bout of courage and determination. He understood the daunting, gruesome task he had to undertake to survive - he had to break the bones in his arm to effectively amputate it.

Fueled by this profound vision, Ralston painstakingly began the process of self-amputation. Using the boulder as a leverage, he snapped the radius and ulna bones of his trapped arm. With a grim determination and a two-inch knife, he began cutting through the tissue and nerves. The pain was unimaginable, the sight grotesque, but the prospect of freedom kept him going.

After over five days of entrapment, Ralston finally staggered out of the canyon, his body emaciated but his spirit indomitable. He had freed himself from the shackles of the boulder but at a severe cost. Finally free, Ralston had to trek miles, bloodied and exhausted, before he was spotted by a family on a helicopter tour. Their chance encounter led to his rescue. This harrowing experience didn't break Ralston, but instead cast him into a symbol of extraordinary human resilience and determination.

Despite the loss of his arm, Ralston emerged from the canyon with a deeper appreciation for life. His story reminds us that we possess an incredible will to survive, a strength that can overcome the most daunting odds. Ralston didn't just escape the canyon, he conquered his circumstances, showing the world that the human spirit is unbreakable. His tale continues to inspire, telling us that in the face of adversity, we too, can find the courage to "cut the boulder loose."

"Don't 'Mine' The Dust - San José copper gold mine - 2010"

On August 5th, 2010, in the San José copper-gold mine near Copiapó, Chile, a catastrophe of unprecedented proportions occurred. Thirty-three miners, ranging in age from 19 to 63, descended into the belly of the Earth for what they believed to be another regular workday. As they penetrated deeper into the 121-year-old mine, a harrowing rumble echoed through the tunnels, followed by a catastrophic collapse of the main ramp. The men found themselves trapped nearly 2300 feet below the surface. The mine had become their prison, and their bid for survival had begun.

The initial cave-in was terrifying. Dust filled the cavernous space, obscuring vision and choking the miners. Once the dust settled, the miners quickly realized the magnitude of their situation: they were trapped, with nearly 700,000 tons of rock between them and the surface. Food supplies were meager, consisting of some tuna, biscuits, peaches, and milk — enough to last them only a couple of days. The dire reality became starkly evident - the battle for survival had begun.

Communication with the outside world was severed. Above ground, the news of the collapse left the miners' families and the rest of the nation in stunned despair. However, hope wasn't completely extinguished. Rescue teams began immediate efforts, drilling exploratory boreholes in an attempt to locate the miners.

Below ground, the trapped miners elected 54-year-old Luis Urzúa as their leader. The shift supervisor was experienced, rational, and known for his cool demeanor under pressure. He rationed the available food to stretch it for as long as possible — one teaspoon of tuna, two biscuits, and half a glass of milk every 48 hours per miner.

In the stifling heat and humidity, with temperatures reaching up to 93 degrees Fahrenheit, days turned into nights and nights into days. Time became an abstract concept as the miners tried to maintain a semblance of normalcy. They followed a routine - work shifts, rest periods, and daily meetings. The miners organized themselves, creating distinct areas for sleeping, waste disposal, and a 'chapel' where daily prayers were held. They kept each other's spirits up, refusing to let despair consume them.

Seventeen days passed without any contact from the outside world. Each exploratory borehole drilled from the surface missed their shelter. Hopes waned. But then, on August 22nd, the drill bit of the eighteenth borehole broke through into their space. A cheer echoed through the mine. The miners attached a note to the drill bit, "Estamos bien en el refugio los 33" – "We are well in the shelter, the 33 of us."

The message sparked joy and relief both in the mine and on the surface. It marked the beginning of a new phase for the miners – the wait for rescue. A lifeline was established with the outside world. Food, water, and letters from loved ones were sent down the borehole. Video conferences with families were arranged, offering the miners emotional support and keeping their hopes alive. The trapped men even watched a live broadcast of a football match - a minor luxury that did wonders for their morale.

Yet, the road to rescue was still a long one. The drilling of the rescue shaft was a complicated and dangerous task. Multiple plans were proposed and scrapped due to the unpredictable and precarious nature of the mine's geology.

Finally, 'Plan B', a high-powered drill typically used to make water wells, began making significant progress. The anticipation grew. Above ground, a custom-built capsule named "Fénix 2" was readied, designed to hoist the miners to safety one at a time.

On October 9th, 65 days after the initial collapse, the drill broke through to the miners' shelter. The rescue shaft was complete. It was a monumental achievement, but the most dangerous part of the operation was about to begin – extracting the miners through the narrow rescue shaft.

On October 12th, the rescue operation began. One by one, the miners were strapped into the Fénix 2 capsule, a narrow steel tube just wide enough to accommodate a man. The first miner to ascend was Florencio Ávalos. As the capsule emerged from the hole, carrying its precious cargo, the world collectively held its breath. Ávalos stepped out of the capsule and into the arms of his waiting family. The cheers of the rescue workers and the relieved sobs of his loved ones echoed into the night. One down, thirty-two to go.

Over the next 24 hours, the capsule made the journey down and up the half-mile rescue shaft 33 times. Miner after miner emerged from the capsule, each greeted by the euphoric applause of the rescue team, the tears and embraces of their loved ones and the cheers of a nation.

The last man to be rescued was Luis Urzúa, the group's leader. As he stepped out of the capsule, the entire rescue site erupted in jubilant celebration. They had done it. After 69 days of entrapment, all 33 miners had been rescued, alive and well.

The story of the 33 Chilean miners is one of extraordinary resilience, unyielding hope, and unparalleled teamwork. It's a tale of men who faced the worst, yet chose to fight, survive, and live. Their courage in the face of dire adversity, their unity in the harshest of circumstances, and their unwavering faith in their rescue serve as an inspiring testament to the human spirit's indomitable will.

Their story is a reminder to us all that even in the darkest tunnels, there is always a ray of hope, and that as long as there is life, there is potential for miracles. In their perseverance, we find the strength to confront our own adversities. We realize that as long as we can hope, we can overcome.

"Heaven to Sea to Hell - Louis Zamperini - 1943"

Louis Zamperini was a man of many virtues - resilience, bravery, and strength beyond measure. Born on January 26, 1917, in Olean, New York, to Italian immigrant parents, Zamperini's life was anything but ordinary. The track and field prodigy had already earned his spot in the sun as an Olympic athlete before he stepped into the shoes of a WWII bombardier. His story is one of survival and indomitable spirit, a testament to the indomitable will of a man in the face of extreme adversity.

As a child, Zamperini was a wild spirit. Often in trouble for fighting and stealing, he was considered a nuisance. However, his older brother, Pete, saw potential in him and channeled his energy into running. Zamperini quickly discovered that he was a natural; his speed was undeniable. By high school, he had set a world interscholastic record for the mile, clocking in at a stunning 4 minutes and 21.2 seconds. The accomplishment earned him a ticket to the 1936 Berlin Olympics. Although he didn't medal, his final lap was so quick that it caught the attention of none other than Adolf Hitler, who requested a personal meeting. The young athlete was making a name for himself.

But as World War II began, Zamperini's life took a drastic turn. The Olympic runner enlisted in the United States Army Air Forces in September 1941, serving as a bombardier in the 372nd Bomb Squadron. His athletic career was set aside as he took on the mantle of a war hero.

On a search and rescue mission on May 27, 1943, Zamperini's plane, the B-24 Liberator named Green Hornet, suffered mechanical failures and crashed into the Pacific Ocean. Of the eleven men onboard, only three, including Zamperini, survived the crash: Pilot Russell Allen 'Phil' Phillips and tail gunner Francis

'Mac' McNamara. They climbed onto a pair of inflatable rafts, with nothing but a few chocolate bars, some fishing line, and their wits to keep them alive.

The days turned into weeks. Lost at sea, they were adrift over 1000 miles from land, fighting off shark attacks, surviving only on rainwater and the raw fish they managed to catch. Yet, Zamperini refused to give in. He maintained an iron discipline, rationing their scarce resources, providing hope, and taking care of Mac, who was badly injured in the crash. They mended their punctured raft, using the canvas from the other as a cover to shield themselves from the scorching sun and freezing nights.

On the 33rd day of their ordeal, Mac succumbed to his injuries, leaving Zamperini and Phillips alone in their struggle against the relentless sea. The two held a brief service for Mac before consigning his body to the deep, a moment that haunted Zamperini in the years to come.

The two remaining survivors endured another fortnight before their situation took a dire turn. On their 47th day at sea, they were picked up by the Japanese Navy. However, rather than salvation, this marked the beginning of a new nightmare. They were taken as prisoners of war, marking the start of a brutal captivity that would last over two years.

Their captors were merciless. Zamperini, the Olympic star turned war hero, was specifically targeted for his fame. He was transported to Kwajalein Atoll and was subjected to excruciating physical and mental torture. His captors didn't just aim to break his body but also his spirit.

The man who orchestrated most of the torture was Mutsuhiro Watanabe, a sadistic guard known as "The Bird" among prisoners. The Bird harbored a specific distaste for Zamperini, focusing on him with a fervor that seemed to go beyond mere cruelty. Watanabe found sadistic pleasure in belittling and physically abusing the once-revered Olympic athlete. He would force Zamperini to race against soldiers, then punish him for winning, or punish the other soldiers for losing. He used the celebrated runner as a symbol to terrorize other POWs.

Still, amidst the routine beatings and starvation, Zamperini held onto the one thing that could not be taken away from him: his spirit. He survived through sheer force of will, drawing upon the inner strength he had honed during his early years of athleticism. The more he was tortured, the more resilient he became. He made secret diaries, shared food rations with fellow prisoners, and did everything he could to keep morale high among his fellow captives.

After two long years of torture and deprivation, the war finally ended. On August 20, 1945, Zamperini and his fellow prisoners were liberated. Although free from captivity, Zamperini bore the physical and emotional scars of his ordeal. Upon returning home, he was hailed as a hero, but he struggled to come to terms with his experiences.

Suffering from post-traumatic stress disorder, Zamperini's life began spiraling out of control. He started drinking excessively and had recurring nightmares of The Bird. But just when it seemed like he was on the verge of collapse, he found salvation in a most unexpected place. At the insistence of his wife, Cynthia, Zamperini attended a sermon by the young evangelist Billy Graham in 1949. It was there that he experienced a profound spiritual awakening.

Guided by his newfound faith, Zamperini took control of his life again. He stopped drinking, his nightmares ceased, and he began to put his life back together. In an incredible act of forgiveness, he even reached out to his former captors, writing letters to many of the guards from his POW days, expressing his forgiveness. He attempted to meet The Bird to forgive him personally, but his former tormentor refused.

In the years that followed, Zamperini channeled his energy into helping troubled youth, establishing the Victory Boys Camp for at-risk teenagers. He wanted to pass on his spirit of resilience and his belief that anyone, no matter what they have suffered, can start anew.

Louis Zamperini's story is a testament to the power of the human spirit. From his youthful days as an Olympic runner to his time as a WWII bombardier, from his horrifying ordeal as a POW to his post-war redemption, Zamperini's life embodies the strength and resilience of the human spirit. His tale is a reminder that even in the face of unimaginable adversity, it is possible not just to survive, but to thrive, and to turn even the most horrific experiences into a source of strength and inspiration.

He once said, "The great lesson of my life is to never give up." This sentiment permeates his incredible journey, reminding us all that no matter how insurmountable the odds may seem, the human spirit can always find a way to triumph.

"Juliane Koepcke's - Triumph Over the Amazon - 1971"

December 24, 1971, began as a day of high anticipation for 17-year-old Juliane Koepcke. She was aboard LANSA Flight 508, traveling with her mother from Lima, Peru, to Pucallpa. Their destination was the remote research station in the Amazon Rainforest, where her father awaited their Christmas reunion. Little did she know, she was about to embark on a harrowing journey of survival that would defy all odds.

The holiday cheer on board was quickly swallowed by a sense of dread as dark, ominous storm clouds began to gather around their aircraft, a Lockheed L-188A Electra turboprop. The plane rattled violently, lurching to the rhythm of the thunderstorm, as flashes of lightning illuminated the terrified faces of the passengers. Despite the pilot's best efforts to navigate the tempest, the plane was struck by a bolt of lightning. The right wing exploded into flames, and the aircraft began a swift, horrifying descent into the heart of the Peruvian Amazon.

As the plane disintegrated around her, Juliane found herself still strapped to her seat, plunging two miles toward the dense rainforest canopy. She blacked out, and when she came to, she was alone in the middle of the jungle, the wreckage of the plane and her mother nowhere in sight. Her descent through the canopy had left her with a broken collarbone, a deep gash in her calf, and an eye swollen shut by a severe concussion. However, it was the realization of her isolation that truly struck terror into her heart.

The Amazon is a place of extreme paradox: it teems with life, yet survival is a constant battle. Juliane was ill-equipped for this test. With only one sandal, a mini dress, and no survival tools, she had to rely on her wits and the knowledge she had gleaned from her parents, both famous zoologists.

Her first instinct was to find her mother, so she spent the initial days after the crash searching the nearby wreckage. As she navigated the difficult terrain, she discovered a bag of sweets, which would serve as her only food during her jungle ordeal.

However, despite her best efforts, her mother remained missing.

As reality set in, Juliane understood she needed to focus on her own survival. She recalled her father's advice about following water downstream in the Amazon to find civilization, so she decided to follow a small brook, hoping it would lead to a larger tributary.

Her journey through the Amazon was fraught with danger at every step. She was faced with relentless rain, swarms of insects, deadly snakes, and treacherous terrain. Her wounds festered and were invaded by maggots, but she pressed on, pushing through the pain and fatigue.

At night, she would huddle on the banks of the brook, plagued by loneliness and fear. She was constantly reminded of the precariousness of her situation by the ever-present growls and calls of jungle predators. Yet, even in the face of despair, she remained tenacious. Every morning, she would pick herself up, wade through the waist-deep water, and continue her journey towards salvation.

On her tenth day in the jungle, Juliane's persistence finally paid off. She found a boat moored near a shelter along the banks of a larger river she had reached. Overwhelmed with relief, she decided to wait for the owner to return. But as the hours passed and nobody came, desperation compelled her to take drastic action.

Relying on a memory of her father tending to a dog's wounds, she used a tube of gasoline she found near the boat to extract the maggots from her arm, wincing as the larvae squirmed out. It was a gruesome task, but one that potentially saved her from a dangerous infection. She then took refuge in the shelter, spending a restless night as she awaited what the next day would bring.

Morning arrived with the sound of human voices. Two local lumbermen had stumbled upon her in their shelter. For Juliane, the sight of these men was akin to seeing a mirage in a desert. They stared at her in disbelief, unable to comprehend how this young girl could have emerged from the Amazon, bruised and battered but unbroken.

Despite their initial shock, the men quickly sprang into action. They treated her wounds, fed her, and even crafted a makeshift stretcher to carry her down the river. They embarked on a seven-hour journey downstream to a lumber station, from where she was airlifted to a missionary hospital in Pucallpa.

At the hospital, Juliane was finally able to tell her tale. News of her incredible survival quickly spread, and she became a symbol of resilience worldwide. However, amidst the frenzy, her heart was heavy with the loss of her mother. It was weeks later that she discovered her mother had initially survived the crash but succumbed to her injuries a few days later.

The pain of losing her mother was immeasurable, but Juliane found strength in the face of tragedy. Her experiences in the Amazon forever shaped her outlook on life. She channeled her ordeal into her studies, later becoming a renowned biologist, just like her parents.

In the years that followed, Juliane returned to the Amazon, the place that had both terrorized her and reinforced her will to survive. She worked tirelessly to preserve its beauty and complexity, using her influence to champion conservation efforts.

Juliane Koepcke's story is one of survival against the steepest odds. It reminds us of the incredible resilience of the human spirit and our innate drive to endure, even in the face of seemingly insurmountable adversity. As she once said, "I had incredible luck — I should have been dead several times. But I always say, if I could survive the Amazon, I can survive anything."

And that she did. Her tale serves as a beacon of inspiration, teaching us that we are capable of far more than we realize, that we can rise from our lowest depths and not just survive, but thrive. It challenges us to find strength within ourselves, to face our fears, and to keep going, no matter how difficult the journey may seem.

For in the end, it is through these trials that we truly discover who we are.

"*Apollo 13 - 1970*"

In the early morning of April 11, 1970, the world watched as the Saturn V rocket pierced the azure Florida sky, carrying with it the hopes and dreams of a nation. Aboard the Apollo 13 spacecraft were three astronauts: Commander Jim Lovell, Command Module Pilot Jack Swigert, and Lunar Module Pilot Fred Haise. The goal of their mission was audacious: to land on the moon and return safely to Earth. Little did they know, they would soon be engaged in a struggle for survival that would test the very limits of human ingenuity and resilience.

Apollo 13's journey began smoothly. As they slipped the bonds of Earth, the crew felt the familiar jolt and rumble of the mighty Saturn V rocket. The systems worked flawlessly, the separation was successful, and soon, the crew found themselves cruising towards the moon. However, as they moved farther away from Earth, they would soon encounter a problem that would turn their routine mission into a desperate fight for survival.

The crisis began on the third day of the mission, April 13th, with a seemingly innocuous request from mission control in Houston: "Apollo 13, we'd like you to stir the cryo tanks." This process involved turning on fans inside the tanks to stir the super-cold liquid oxygen, a standard procedure to prevent stratification. Jack Swigert toggled the switch.

Suddenly, the astronauts heard a loud 'bang,' followed by a shudder that echoed through the spacecraft. Alarm lights began flashing, and the astronauts could see a decrease in the readings from the number two oxygen tank. Within moments, the trio realized they were in serious trouble.

As the reality of their situation set in, the now-famous phrase was calmly relayed to Mission Control: "Houston, we've had a problem here." It was an understatement of cosmic proportions. An explosion had ruptured the oxygen tank in the service module, crippling the spacecraft's life-support system and propulsion.

Back on Earth, in Mission Control, Flight Director Gene Kranz swiftly

gathered his team to assess the situation. The mood was tense. An air

of grave concern hung over the room as the magnitude of the disaster

sank in. Their task was immense; they needed to bring the astronauts

home safely using a crippled spacecraft over 200,000 miles from Earth.

The lunar landing was quickly abandoned, and the focus turned towards

survival. The ground team devised an ingenious plan to loop the

spacecraft around the moon, using the lunar gravity to propel the

spacecraft back towards Earth.

Meanwhile, on the crippled Apollo 13, the situation was growing dire.

The explosion had knocked out their main source of electricity, light, and

life-supporting systems. The temperature dropped near freezing, and the

spaceship grew damp. Their water supply was limited, dehydration

threatened, and the risk of a dangerous build-up of carbon dioxide was

increasing.

However, the crew maintained their poise under these challenging

conditions. The ground team swiftly came up with a plan to adapt the

command module's square carbon dioxide scrubbers to fit the round

holes in the lunar module using only materials available on board like duct tape, plastic bags, and cardboard. The crew followed their instructions, and the improvised 'mailbox' was a success. The carbon dioxide levels started to drop. It was a crucial victory, a testament to human ingenuity and resilience under pressure.

Yet, the ordeal was far from over. The journey back to Earth was fraught with difficulties. A critical engine burn needed to be executed to keep them on the right trajectory. Without their computer systems, the crew relied on the Earth as their guiding star, manually controlling the spacecraft for a critical 14-second burn. The tension was palpable, but their execution was flawless, a testament to their exceptional training and unwavering focus.

During the final leg of their journey, the crew transferred back into the command module for re-entry. The lunar module, their lifeboat, was jettisoned, and they saw for the first time the extent of the damage. An entire panel of the service module had been blown off; it was a chilling sight, a stark reminder of the catastrophe they had endured.

Re-entry was the final hurdle. The command module, the only part of the Apollo 13 spacecraft that was intended to return to Earth, was designed to withstand the intense heat generated by friction against the Earth's atmosphere. But the explosion had occurred near the heat shield, and if it had been damaged, the consequences would be catastrophic.

As Apollo 13 began its descent, it was enveloped by ionized gases that caused a communication blackout, expected to last for about three minutes. Those were possibly the longest three minutes in the annals of space exploration, with the team at mission control and people worldwide holding their breaths, awaiting the crew's safe return.

Three minutes passed, then four, and still, there was no communication from Apollo 13. Just as the fear was turning into a grim certainty, the static crackled to life. "Houston, this is Odyssey. It's good to see you again." A wave of relief washed over mission control. Apollo 13 had made it through the atmosphere.

On April 17, 1970, the command module splashed down in the Pacific Ocean near Samoa. The ordeal of Apollo 13 ended with the safe return of its crew, against all odds. As the world celebrated, the three astronauts, weary but unbroken, gave silent thanks for their deliverance.

The Apollo 13 mission is remembered not as a failed lunar landing, but as a successful demonstration of human ingenuity, teamwork, and resilience. Despite being faced with an unprecedented crisis in the unforgiving environment of space, the team on the ground and the crew aboard Apollo 13 showed unyielding resolve, transforming potential disaster into a 'successful failure.'

After the mission, Gene Kranz, the lead flight director, was quoted as saying, "I was sick to my stomach with an unspeakable emptiness." But he also added, "From this day forward, Flight Control will be known by two words: 'Tough' and 'Competent.' Tough meaning we will never again shirk from our responsibility, and competent meaning we'll never again take anything for granted."

The saga of Apollo 13 serves as a reminder that even in the face of terrifying uncertainty and potential disaster, humanity can rise to the occasion. It is a testament to our capacity to innovate, collaborate, and persevere, no matter the odds.

The story of Apollo 13 resonates far beyond the realms of space exploration. It serves as a beacon of inspiration, illuminating the power of human resilience, the strength of teamwork, and the unyielding spirit that allows us to turn perilous journeys into triumphant returns. It teaches us that, even when we venture into the unknown, as long as we remain 'tough' and 'competent,' we can face any challenge that comes our way

and make it safely home.

"As you turn this final page and reflect on the tales of resilience you've just journeyed through, remember this: every story you've read is a testament to the strength and endurance of the human spirit. They are stark reminders that no matter the adversity faced, no matter how insurmountable the obstacle might seem, there is always a path forward, a path to overcome and thrive. You've read about individuals who defied the odds, who triumphed in the face of immense hardships. It's easy to think of these people as extraordinary, as heroes, and they are. But remember, at their core, they are just like you. They are humans who were tested by life and chose not to give up, chose to fight, chose to overcome. These stories were not just meant to be read and forgotten. They are a call to action. A call for you to tap into your own wellspring of resilience, to defy your own odds, and to overcome your own trials. No matter what challenges you're facing, remember there's a wealth of strength within you, waiting to be unleashed."

I hope you enjoyed reading this as much as I enjoyed writing it.

George